MY BIRD

Me and My
PET

By William Anthony

KidHaven
PUBLISHING

Published in 2020 by KidHaven Publishing, an Imprint of Greenhaven Publishing, LLC
353 3rd Avenue, Suite 255, New York, NY 10010

Written by: William Anthony
Edited by: Madeline Tyler
Designed by: Jasmine Pointer

Cataloging-in-Publication Data

Names: Anthony, William.
Title: My bird / William Anthony.
Description: New York : KidHaven Publishing, 2020. | Series: Me and my pet | Includes glossary and index.
Identifiers: ISBN 9781534533295 (pbk.) | ISBN 9781534533318 (library bound) | ISBN 9781534533301 (6 pack) | ISBN 9781534533325 (ebook)
Subjects: LCSH: Birds--Juvenile literature. | Cage birds--Juvenile literature.
Classification: LCC QL676.2 A58 2020 | DDC 636.6'8--dc23

Photo credits: Images are courtesy of Shutterstock.com. With thanks to Getty Images, Thinkstock Photo and iStockphoto.
Front cover - Stephen Denness, iLight photo. 2 - izlverichka. 3 - VitCOM Photo, Sondre Lysne. 4 - Stephen Denness, Feng Yu. 5 - Africa Studio.
6 - waldru. 7 - You Touch Pix of EuToch. 8 - Stephen Denness. 9 - VitCOM Photo. 10 - VladimirMPetrov. 11 - photomaster. 12 - Julia_585.
13 - Kolotygin Igor. 14 - fon.tepsoda. 15 - Artex67. 16 - Katerina Graghine. 17 - hedgehog94. 18 - Kolotygin Igor. 19 - Santhosh Varghese.
20 - Ramona Edwards. 21 - Ramona Edwards. 22 - Stephen Denness. 23 - Vyaseleva Elena.

Printed in the United States of America

CPSIA compliance information: Batch #BW20KL: For further information contact Greenhaven Publishing LLC, New York, New York at 1-844-317-7404.

CONTENTS

Words that look like this can be found in the glossary on page 24.

Tom ♥ and Sky

Hello! My name's Tom, and this is my pet bird, Sky. She's four years old. Birds are my favorite animal because they whistle and make funny noises.

Tom

Sky

Whether you're thinking about getting a bird, or you've had one for a little while, Sky and I are going to take you through how to look after your feathered friend.

Lead the way, Sky!

Getting a Bird

Looking after a bird means you are going to have a lot of _responsibility_. You will need to feed them and give them a nice home with lots of toys.

My family got Sky from a <u>rescue center</u>, but you can also get birds from some pet shops or a breeder. A breeder is someone who keeps birds to <u>mate</u> them.

Always make sure you <u>research</u> the person or place you're buying a pet from.

Home

Your new bird should be kept in a large cage with lots of room for them to stretch out their wings and move around.

There are a few important things you need to put in your bird's cage. They need a place to get food and water, a small birdbath to wash in, and lots of fun toys!

A birdbath will help your bird keep itself clean.

Playtime

Speaking of toys, birds need lots of things in their cage to keep them happy. You could put in a climbing rope, a ladder, or even a little swing!

10

You can also let your bird out of their cage to fly around. You should only do this if your bird is tame. Having a chance to flap their wings will keep your bird very happy!

Make sure you close doors and windows and make the room safe first!

11

Fod

You need to
feed your bird a
balanced and healthy **diet**.
You can buy bird food from any
pet shop. Bird food is made up
of lots of different seeds.

You can also give your bird lots of different treats. These can be things such as grapes, carrots, and apples. You can even use these to train your bird to do tricks!

Treats help birds to know when they've done a trick well.

Bedtime ᶻᶻᶻ

Sometimes birds sleep standing on just one leg!

Some birds are awake during the day and asleep during the night, just like people. However, birds don't lie down to sleep. They sleep standing up!

Your bird will need a perch to stand on while they sleep. They need to be in a quiet place in your house so they don't get woken up.

Zzzzz!

Some birds will also like a night light, just like people!

The Vet

Vets are doctors, but for animals instead of humans!

Birds can get sick, just like humans. Birds that are sick can go see the vet. The vet will do everything they can to help your bird get better again!

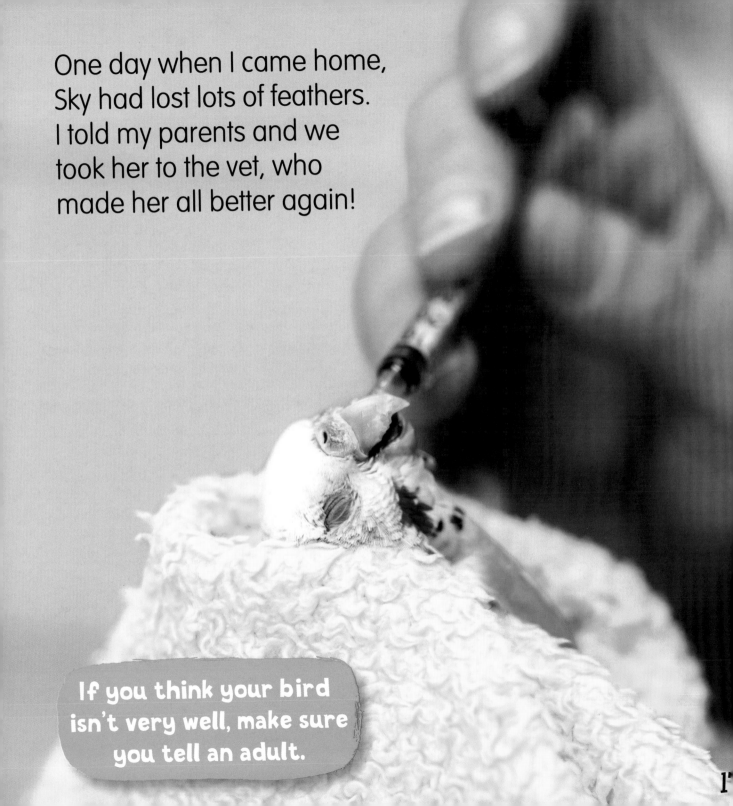

One day when I came home, Sky had lost lots of feathers. I told my parents and we took her to the vet, who made her all better again!

If you think your bird isn't very well, make sure you tell an adult.

Growing Up

As your bird grows up, it might start to sleep more and eat less. You don't need to worry. Your bird might just be getting older.

There are things you can do to make life easier for your elderly bird. If you make sure their room is always warm and quiet, they will be very happy in their old age!

Be very calm and gentle when you're petting an old bird.

Super Birds

Birds have many hidden talents. Some birds are simply super! Disco is a bird from the U.S., and he has learned how to mimic a lot of human words.

Some birds can mimic human voices, but Disco can remember over 130 sentences. He can demand cheeseburgers, quote famous films, and sing songs!

You ❤ and Your Pet

Your bird might not talk, but they will be special to you, so make sure you take care of them just like Sky and I have taught you!

I'm sure you'll make a great pet owner. Try to think of some tricks you could teach your new bird. Most of all, enjoy spending time with your new feathered friend!

GLOSSARY

balanced	having good or equal amounts of something
diet	the kinds of food that an animal or person usually eats
mate	to produce young with an animal of the same species
mimic	to copy something or someone
rescue center	a place that helps animals that have had a difficult life find a new home
research	the activity of getting information about a subject
responsibility	having tasks that you are expected to do
tame	trained to do what it's told

INDEX